CONTENTS

INTRODUCTION

❖ ❖ ❖

Deception is a word that has always been associated with negative connotations. It is seen as a tool for manipulation, lying, and dishonesty. However, what if we told you that deception can also be used in a positive and healthy way? That is precisely what this book is all about.

In this book, we will explore the art of deception and how it can be used as a healthy tactic. We will look at different types of deception, including lying, bluffing, and strategic misrepresentation, and discuss their potential benefits and drawbacks. We will also examine the ethical considerations that come with using deception and provide practical tips on how to use it effectively and ethically.

Contrary to popular belief, deception can be used for good. It can help protect privacy, preserve social harmony, and advance society. Moreover, it can be a valuable tool in personal and professional relationships, business negotiations, and even politics.

However, it is crucial to use deception in a healthy and ethical way. We must be aware of its potential risks and consequences, and we must always consider the long-term effects of our actions.

If you are looking to expand your knowledge of the art of deception, or if you are interested in using it as a healthy tactic, then this book is for you. It offers a unique perspective on the subject, highlighting its positive aspects, while also providing practical advice on how to use it effectively and ethically. By the end of this book, you will have a comprehensive understanding of the art of deception and how it can benefit you in your personal and professional life.

EXPLANATION OF THE CONCEPT OF DECEPTION

◆ ◆ ◆

Deception is a complex and multifaceted concept that has been studied extensively in various fields, including psychology, sociology, philosophy, and communication studies. At its core, deception involves deliberately misleading others by providing false or misleading information.

Deception can take many different forms, ranging from outright lies to strategic misrepresentation. Lying is perhaps the most common form of deception, and it involves intentionally saying something that is not true. For example, a person might lie about their whereabouts, their actions, or their feelings in order to avoid getting in trouble or to manipulate others.

Another form of deception is bluffing, which involves making false claims or threats in order to gain an advantage in a particular situation. For example, a poker player might bluff about having a strong hand in order to scare their opponents into folding their cards.

Strategic misrepresentation is a more subtle form of deception, which involves intentionally conveying information in a way that is misleading or ambiguous. For example, a politician might use carefully crafted language to suggest that they support a particular policy without actually committing to it.

While deception is often seen as a negative and harmful behavior, it can also be used in a positive and healthy way. For example, deception can help protect privacy by allowing individuals to withhold information that they do not want to share. It can also help preserve social harmony by allowing individuals to avoid conflict or maintain relationships.

In addition, deception can be a valuable tool in personal and professional relationships, allowing individuals to negotiate and compromise in a way that benefits both parties. Moreover, deception can be used to advance society by allowing individuals to strategically communicate and promote their ideas in a way that is persuasive and effective.

However, it is important to note that deception can also have negative consequences. It can erode trust and undermine the integrity of relationships, and it can cause harm to individuals and society. In addition, deception can have legal consequences, such as fraud or perjury.

In conclusion, deception is a complex and multifaceted concept that can be both positive and negative. While it can be used as a healthy tactic in certain situations, it is important to use it ethically and with careful consideration of its potential risks and consequences. By understanding the concept of deception and its various forms, individuals can make informed decisions about when and how to use it effectively in their personal and professional lives.

BRIEF OVERVIEW OF THE PROS AND CONS OF DECEPTION

* * *

Deception is a complex and controversial topic that has been the subject of much debate in various fields, including psychology, philosophy, and communication studies. While there are certainly advantages and disadvantages to using deception, it is important to recognize that the effects of deception are highly situational and depend on the context in which it is used.

One of the main advantages of deception is that it can be used to protect privacy and avoid conflict. For example, if a person does not want to disclose personal information to someone, they may choose to deceive that person in order to protect their privacy. Similarly, in situations where a conflict could escalate, deception may be used to avoid confrontation and maintain social harmony.

Deception can also be a valuable tool in negotiation and bargaining. In business negotiations, for example, a negotiator may use deception to gain leverage and secure a better deal. Similarly, in personal relationships, deception can help individuals to compromise and find mutually beneficial solutions.

However, the use of deception also carries significant risks and potential negative consequences. One of the main drawbacks of deception is that it can erode trust and undermine the integrity of relationships. If individuals are caught in a lie or otherwise deceived, it can damage their credibility and make it difficult to build trust in the future.

Moreover, deception can have legal

consequences. In cases of fraud or perjury, for example, the use of deception can result in serious legal penalties. Deception can also cause harm to individuals and society, particularly in cases where it is used to manipulate or exploit vulnerable individuals.

In conclusion, while there are certainly advantages and disadvantages to using deception, it is important to recognize that the effects of deception are highly situational and context-dependent. While it can be a valuable tool in certain situations, it is important to use deception ethically and with careful consideration of its potential risks and consequences. By understanding the pros and cons of deception, individuals can make informed decisions about when and how to use it effectively in their personal and professional lives.

IMPORTANCE OF USING DECEPTION EFFECTIVELY AND ETHICALLY

◆ ◆ ◆

Deception can be a powerful tool in many areas of life, from personal relationships to business negotiations. However, it is important to use deception effectively and ethically, in order to avoid negative consequences and maintain trust and credibility.

One of the key reasons to use deception effectively and ethically is to protect relationships and social connections. Deception that is uncovered or perceived as malicious can harm relationships and damage social connections. As humans, we rely on trust to build relationships and connect with others. When trust is broken or betrayed through deception, it can be difficult to rebuild or restore these relationships.

In addition, using deception effectively and ethically can help to avoid negative consequences. When deception is used to manipulate, exploit or deceive others for personal gain, it can cause harm to individuals and society. Deceptive practices such as fraud or embezzlement can lead to legal and financial consequences that can impact the individual and the wider community.

Another reason to use deception effectively and ethically is to promote fairness and equity. When deception is used to gain an unfair advantage, it can undermine the principles of fairness and equity. For example, if a business uses deceptive practices to gain market share or eliminate competitors, it can create an unfair advantage that harms other businesses and consumers.

Using deception effectively and ethically also promotes personal and professional growth. When individuals use deception in a thoughtful and strategic manner, they can develop their negotiation and communication skills. They can learn to navigate complex situations and find mutually beneficial solutions. Ethical and effective use of deception can also foster trust, build relationships, and strengthen connections with others.

In conclusion, it is important to use deception effectively and ethically, in order to avoid negative consequences and maintain trust and credibility. Using deception thoughtfully and strategically can promote fairness, equity, personal and professional growth, and positive social connections. By understanding the importance of ethical and effective use of deception, individuals can make informed decisions about when and how to use deception in their personal and professional lives.

TYPES OF DECEPTION

Lying

Lying is a common and complex form of deception that has been the subject of much discussion and debate in many fields, including psychology, philosophy, and communication studies. While lying can have both positive and negative effects, it is important to recognize that it carries significant risks and potential negative consequences.

One of the main reasons why people lie is to protect themselves or others from harm. In some cases, lying can help individuals avoid negative consequences, such as punishment or social exclusion. Lying can also be used to protect others from harm, such as when a person tells a lie to protect a friend from criticism or negative attention.

However, lying can also have serious negative consequences. One of the main drawbacks of lying is that it can erode trust and undermine relationships. When people lie, they can damage their credibility and make it difficult to build trust in the future. In personal relationships, lying can cause emotional harm and lead to the breakdown of the relationship. In professional relationships, lying can damage reputations and lead to legal and financial consequences.

Moreover, lying can also have psychological consequences. When people lie, they can experience feelings of guilt, shame, and anxiety. Chronic lying can lead to a pattern of dishonesty that can be difficult to break. This can impact a person's mental health and lead to social isolation and other negative outcomes.

In addition, lying can have societal consequences. When lying is used to manipulate or deceive others for personal gain, it can cause harm to individuals and society. Lying can be used to spread false information or propaganda, which can have significant negative consequences on a societal level.

In conclusion, while lying can have both positive and negative effects, it is important to recognize that it carries significant risks and potential negative consequences. Lying can erode trust and undermine relationships, lead to psychological consequences, and cause harm to individuals and society. By understanding the risks and consequences of lying, individuals can make informed decisions about when and how to use deception in their personal and professional lives. It is important to approach lying with caution and use it only in situations where it is necessary and ethical.

Different types of lies

Lying is a complex phenomenon that takes many forms and has many motivations.

Understanding the different types of lies can help us to better understand the reasons why people lie and the impact that lying can have on individuals and society. Here are some of the different types of lies:

White lies: White lies are often seen as harmless lies that are told to avoid hurting someone's feelings or to maintain social harmony. For example, telling a friend that they look good in an outfit even if you don't really think so, or telling a colleague that their presentation was great even if it wasn't. While white lies are often seen as benign, they can still erode trust and have negative consequences.

Pathological lies: Pathological lies are lies that are told compulsively, often without any clear motivation or gain. Pathological liars may lie about everything from their personal experiences to their accomplishments and abilities. Pathological lying can be a symptom of a larger mental health issue, such as borderline personality disorder or narcissistic personality disorder.

Omission lies: Omission lies involve leaving

out important information or failing to disclose relevant details. For example, not telling a partner about a past relationship, or failing to disclose a conflict of interest in a professional setting. Omission lies can be just as damaging as outright lies, as they can undermine trust and credibility.

Self-serving lies: Self-serving lies are lies that are told to benefit oneself. For example, exaggerating accomplishments on a resume, or lying to avoid punishment or negative consequences. Self-serving lies can have significant negative consequences, as they can lead to legal and financial consequences and harm personal and professional relationships.

Deceptive lies: Deceptive lies involve intentionally misleading someone for personal gain or advantage. Deceptive lies can be used in business, politics, or personal relationships to gain an unfair advantage or manipulate others. Deceptive lies can cause significant harm to individuals and society, as they can undermine trust and lead to negative consequences.

In conclusion, lying takes many forms and has many motivations. While some lies may seem harmless, all lies have the potential to erode trust and have negative consequences. Understanding the different types of lies can help us to better understand the reasons why people lie and how to navigate situations where deception may be present. It is important to approach lying with caution and use it only in situations where it is necessary and ethical.

Benefits and drawbacks of lying

Lying is a complex phenomenon that can have both positive and negative effects, depending on the situation and motivation behind the lie. While lying can sometimes be seen as a necessary tool for achieving certain goals, it is important to recognize that it carries significant risks and potential negative consequences. Here are some of the benefits and drawbacks of lying:

Benefits of lying

Avoiding negative consequences: One of the

main reasons why people lie is to avoid negative consequences, such as punishment or social exclusion. Lying can be used to protect oneself or others from harm, such as when a person lies to protect a friend from criticism or negative attention.

Achieving personal gain: Lying can also be used to achieve personal gain or advantage, such as when a person lies on a job application to get hired, or when a politician lies to gain public support.

Protecting privacy: Lying can be used to protect one's privacy or personal information, such as when a person lies about their age or income to avoid sharing sensitive information.

Drawbacks of lying

Eroding trust: Lying can erode trust and undermine relationships, both on a personal and professional level. When people lie, they can damage their credibility and make it difficult to build trust in the future.

Damaging reputation: Lying can also damage reputations and lead to legal and financial consequences. If a person is caught lying, it can have significant negative consequences on their personal and professional life.

Causing emotional harm: Lying can cause emotional harm and lead to the breakdown of relationships. When people lie, it can cause feelings of betrayal, anger, and hurt, which can be difficult to repair.

Impacting mental health: Chronic lying can lead to a pattern of dishonesty that can be difficult to break. This can impact a person's mental health and lead to social isolation and other negative outcomes.

In conclusion, while lying can sometimes be seen as a necessary tool for achieving certain goals, it is important to recognize that it carries significant risks and potential negative consequences. Lying can erode trust, damage reputations, cause emotional harm, and impact mental health. By understanding the benefits and drawbacks of lying, individuals can make informed decisions about when and how to use deception in their personal and professional lives. It is important to approach lying with caution and use it only in situations where it is necessary and ethical.

Bluffing

Bluffing is a strategy that involves deceiving others by pretending to have something that you do not have or by misleading them about your intentions or actions. It is commonly used in games of strategy, such as poker and chess, as well as in business negotiations and other competitive situations.

There are several benefits to bluffing. For example, it can be an effective way to gain an advantage over opponents, especially when they are uncertain about your intentions. Bluffing can also be a way to avoid negative outcomes, such as losing a game or facing consequences in a negotiation.

However, there are also drawbacks to bluffing. One of the main risks of bluffing is that it can be difficult to maintain the deception over time. Once your opponents become aware of your bluffing tactics, they may be able to adapt their strategies accordingly, which can make it more difficult to succeed in future situations.

Another potential drawback of bluffing is that it can damage your reputation and credibility if you are caught. If your opponents discover that you have been bluffing, they may be less likely to trust you in the future, which can make it more difficult to build effective relationships and negotiate successfully.

Despite these risks, bluffing can still be a useful strategy when used effectively and ethically. By carefully considering the situation and the potential risks and benefits of bluffing, individuals can make informed decisions about when and how to use this strategy to achieve their goals.

Overall, bluffing is a complex strategy that requires careful consideration and effective execution. While it can be a powerful way to gain an advantage in competitive situations, it also carries significant risks and potential negative consequences. By weighing the pros and cons of bluffing and using this strategy ethically, individuals can improve their chances of success in a wide range of situations.

How bluffing works

Bluffing is a strategy that involves deceiving others by pretending to have something that you do not have or by misleading them about your intentions or actions. This strategy can be used in a variety of contexts, including games of strategy, business negotiations, and social interactions.

At its core, bluffing works by exploiting uncertainty and exploiting the tendency of others to make assumptions based on incomplete information. By carefully managing the information that is available to others and using subtle cues and signals, a bluffer can create the impression that they have something that they do not actually possess.

In games of strategy, bluffing often involves pretending to have a stronger hand than you actually do. For example, in poker, a player may raise the bet even if they have a weak hand, in order to create the impression that they have a strong hand and intimidate their opponents into folding. Similarly, in chess, a player may make a feint or sacrifice a piece in order to mislead their opponent and gain a strategic advantage.

In business negotiations, bluffing can involve making false claims about the value of a product or service, or misleading your opponent about your willingness to walk away from the negotiation. By creating the impression that you have more leverage or a stronger position than you actually do, you can gain an advantage and secure a better outcome.

Bluffing can also be used in social interactions, such as when a person pretends to be more confident or successful than they actually are. By projecting an image of confidence and success, a person can gain social status and influence, even if their actual accomplishments are more modest.

In order for bluffing to work effectively, it is important to manage the information that is available to others and to use subtle cues and signals to convey your intentions. This may involve controlling your facial expressions, tone of voice, and body language in order to create the desired impression.

In conclusion, bluffing is a powerful strategy that can be used in a variety of contexts to gain an advantage over others. By exploiting uncertainty and manipulating information, a bluffer can create the impression of strength and confidence, even if their actual position is weaker. However, bluffing also carries risks and potential negative consequences, such as damage to your reputation and credibility if you are caught. As such, it is important to use bluffing judiciously and ethically, and to carefully weigh the potential risks and benefits of this strategy in each situation.

Examples of bluffing in different contexts

Bluffing is a versatile strategy that can be used in a wide range of contexts, including games of strategy, business negotiations, and social interactions. Here are a few examples of bluffing in different contexts:

Games of Strategy: One of the most well-known examples of bluffing in games of strategy is in poker. In this game, players can bluff by pretending to have a stronger hand than they actually do, in order to intimidate their opponents into folding. For example, a player may raise the bet even if they have a weak hand, in order to create the impression that they have a strong hand and discourage others from challenging them.

Business Negotiations: Bluffing can also be used in business negotiations, particularly when it comes to pricing and terms. For example, a salesperson may exaggerate the value of a product or service in order to create the impression that it is more valuable than it actually is. Similarly, a negotiator may threaten to walk away from the negotiation even if they are willing to compromise, in order to create the impression that they have more leverage than they actually do.

Social Interactions: Bluffing can also be used in social interactions, particularly when it comes to projecting confidence and status. For example, a person may exaggerate their accomplishments or present a false image of success in order to impress others and gain social status. Similarly, a person may feign confidence even if they are feeling uncertain or nervous, in order to create the impression that they are in control of the situation.

Sports: Bluffing can also be used in sports to gain an advantage over opponents. In basketball, for example, a player may make a fake shot in order to mislead their opponent and gain a better position for a real shot. Similarly, in soccer, a player may pretend to take a shot in order to draw defenders away from the goal and create space for a teammate to score.

Overall, bluffing is a versatile strategy that can be used in a variety of contexts to gain an advantage over others. While it carries risks and potential negative consequences, it can also be a powerful tool when used effectively and ethically. By carefully considering the situation and the potential risks and benefits of bluffing, individuals can make informed decisions about when and how to use this strategy to achieve their goals.

Strategic Misrepresentation

Strategic misrepresentation is the act of intentionally presenting false or misleading information for strategic advantage in a given situation. This can take many forms, including lying, exaggerating, and omitting important information. While strategic misrepresentation can be an effective tactic in some situations, it also carries significant risks and ethical considerations.

One of the primary benefits of strategic misrepresentation is that it can give individuals or organizations a strategic advantage in negotiations, competitions, or other interactions. By presenting false or misleading information, they can manipulate the perceptions and actions of others, ultimately leading to a more favorable outcome for themselves. For example, a job candidate may exaggerate their qualifications in order to secure a job offer, or a business may misrepresent their financial performance to attract investors.

However, there are also significant drawbacks to using strategic misrepresentation. One of the most obvious is the risk of being caught. If the deception is discovered, it can lead to significant damage to one's reputation, relationships, and legal or financial consequences. In some cases, it may also be illegal, leading to criminal charges or civil lawsuits.

Additionally, strategic misrepresentation can be ethically problematic. It involves intentionally misleading others, which can violate principles of honesty and integrity. In some cases, it can also be harmful to others. For example, misrepresenting the safety or efficacy of a product can lead to harm or injury to consumers.

Despite these drawbacks, strategic

misrepresentation continues to be a common tactic in many contexts. To use this strategy effectively and ethically, individuals and organizations must carefully consider the potential risks and benefits, as well as the ethical implications of their actions. They should also strive to maintain transparency and honesty whenever possible, and avoid misrepresenting information unless it is truly necessary for achieving their goals.

In conclusion, strategic misrepresentation can be an effective tactic for gaining a strategic advantage in certain situations. However, it carries significant risks and ethical considerations, and should only be used with careful consideration and caution. Ultimately, the key to using strategic misrepresentation effectively and ethically is to balance the potential benefits with the potential drawbacks, and to act with honesty and integrity whenever possible.

Examples of strategic misrepresentation

Strategic misrepresentation is a tactic that can take many forms, and it is used in a variety of contexts to gain a strategic advantage. Here are some examples of how strategic misrepresentation can be used in different situations:

Business: Companies may misrepresent their financial performance to attract investors or secure loans. For example, they may inflate their revenue or understate their expenses to make their financial statements appear more favorable than they actually are.

Politics: Politicians may misrepresent their opponent's positions or record to gain an advantage in an election. They may also exaggerate their own accomplishments or qualifications to appeal to voters.

Negotiations: In negotiations, parties may misrepresent their bargaining position or their willingness to compromise in order to gain a better deal. They may also withhold important information or make false promises to convince the other party to agree to their terms.

Advertising: Advertisers may misrepresent the benefits or features of a product to make it appear more appealing to consumers. For example, they may use misleading statistics or exaggerate the product's effectiveness to convince consumers to make a purchase.

Job interviews: Job candidates may misrepresent their qualifications or experience to secure a job offer. They may also downplay their weaknesses or inflate their accomplishments to make themselves appear more qualified than they actually are.

Personal relationships: In personal relationships, individuals may misrepresent their intentions or feelings in order to manipulate the other person. For example, they may lie about their romantic interest or pretend to share the other person's values in order to gain their trust.

While strategic misrepresentation can be an effective tactic in these and other contexts, it is important to consider the potential risks and ethical implications of using it.

When misrepresentation is discovered, it can lead to significant damage to one's reputation and relationships, and may even result in legal or financial consequences. Therefore, individuals and organizations must carefully consider the potential risks and benefits of using strategic misrepresentation, and should strive to act with honesty and integrity whenever possible.

Ethical considerations

Ethical considerations are a critical aspect of decision-making in all areas of life. When it comes to deception and strategic misrepresentation, ethical considerations are particularly important. Here are some of the key ethical considerations that individuals and organizations should take into account when engaging in these practices:

Honesty: Honesty is a fundamental ethical principle, and it is essential for maintaining trust and credibility in personal and professional relationships. Deception and strategic misrepresentation involve intentionally misleading others, which goes against the principle of honesty.

Fairness: Fairness is another important ethical principle, and it requires that individuals treat others equitably and avoid taking advantage of them unfairly. Strategic misrepresentation can be seen as unfair when it is used to gain an unfair advantage or to manipulate others.

Responsibility: Responsibility involves taking accountability for one's actions and the consequences that result from them. Deception and strategic misrepresentation can have significant consequences, and it is important for individuals and organizations to take responsibility for the impact of their actions.

Respect: Respect involves treating others with dignity and recognizing their inherent worth. Deception and strategic misrepresentation can be seen as disrespectful when they involve manipulating or exploiting others for personal gain.

Transparency: Transparency involves being open and honest about one's actions and intentions. Deception and strategic misrepresentation involve hiding information or misrepresenting the truth, which goes against the principle of transparency.

While deception and strategic misrepresentation can be effective tactics in certain situations, it is important for individuals and organizations to consider the ethical implications of these practices. This means weighing the potential benefits against the potential harm, considering the impact on others, and striving to act with honesty, fairness, responsibility, respect, and transparency whenever possible. By doing so, individuals and organizations can maintain trust, credibility, and integrity in all their relationships and endeavors.

THE PROS OF DECEPTION

◆ ◆ ◆

Protection of privacy

Deception is a tactic that can be used to achieve various goals, both personal and professional. While it is often associated with negative connotations, such as dishonesty and unethical behavior, there are also pros to the use of deception. One of the significant pros of deception is its ability to protect privacy.

In today's digital age, privacy has become a significant concern. With the increasing use of technology, individuals are sharing more personal information than ever before. This information can be used to target them with personalized ads or even to commit identity theft. Deception can be used to protect privacy by keeping personal information out of the hands of those who would use it for nefarious purposes.

For example, a person may use deception to protect their online privacy by using a fake name or email address. This tactic can help prevent their personal information from being shared with third-party companies or hackers. Similarly, companies may use deception to protect customer data by using encryption or other security measures to prevent unauthorized access.

Another way deception can protect privacy is by preventing unwanted intrusion into personal space. For instance, a person may use deception to avoid answering unwanted questions from a nosy neighbor or coworker. By misleading the person, the individual can maintain their privacy and keep their personal information secure.

In conclusion, while deception may have negative connotations, it can also be a useful tool for protecting privacy. By using deception effectively and ethically, individuals and organizations can safeguard their personal information and prevent unwanted intrusion into their personal space. Ultimately, the pros of deception can be harnessed to achieve desirable outcomes while minimizing harm to oneself and others.

Preservation of social harmony

Deception is often associated with negative connotations, such as dishonesty and unethical behavior. However, there are also pros to the use of deception, including the preservation of social harmony. Social harmony refers to the peaceful and cooperative coexistence of individuals within a society. Deception can be used as a tool to promote social harmony by avoiding conflict and maintaining positive relationships.

In interpersonal relationships, deception can be used to avoid hurting someone's feelings or causing unnecessary conflict. For example, a person may deceive their friend by telling them they have a prior engagement to avoid attending an event they are not interested in attending. This deception can help preserve the friendship by preventing a potentially awkward or unpleasant situation.

In a broader societal context, deception can be used to prevent conflict and maintain social order. For instance, a government may use deception to prevent social unrest or to avoid a potential crisis. In this context, deception can be seen as a necessary means to maintain social stability and promote the greater good.

Deception can also be used to promote social harmony by promoting cooperation and collaboration. For example, a negotiator may use deception to facilitate a deal that is beneficial to all parties involved. By presenting a false position or intention, the negotiator can encourage the other party to make concessions that ultimately benefit both sides.

In conclusion, while deception may have negative connotations, it can also be a useful tool for promoting social harmony.

By using deception effectively and ethically, individuals and organizations can avoid conflict, maintain positive relationships, and promote cooperation and collaboration. Ultimately, the pros of deception can be harnessed to achieve desirable outcomes while minimizing harm to oneself and others.

Personal and professional gain

Deception can be used as a tool to achieve personal and professional goals by manipulating information and perceptions.

In personal relationships, deception can be used to protect oneself or gain an advantage. For instance, a person may deceive their romantic partner by hiding their true feelings or actions in order to avoid conflict or maintain control in the relationship. This deception can help the individual achieve their personal goals or protect themselves from harm.

In the professional world, deception can be used to gain a competitive advantage or protect one's business interests. For example, a business may deceive their competitors by presenting false information or concealing their true plans to gain an advantage in the market. This deception can help the business achieve their professional goals and protect their interests from competitors.

Deception can also be used to gain personal or professional recognition and success. In some cases, individuals may exaggerate their achievements or credentials in order to gain respect and admiration from others. This deception can help the individual achieve personal or professional goals by increasing their reputation and opportunities for advancement.

In conclusion, while deception may have negative connotations, it can also be a useful tool for achieving personal and professional gain. By using deception effectively and ethically, individuals can protect themselves, gain a competitive advantage, and achieve personal and professional success. However, it is important to recognize that deception can have negative consequences if used improperly or unethically. It is important to consider the potential harm to oneself and others before engaging in deceptive practices.

Advancement of society

Deception can also have positive effects on the advancement of society. In some cases, deception can be used to protect individuals or society as a whole, leading to progress and innovation.

For example, during times of war, deception can be used to mislead the enemy and protect the lives of soldiers and civilians. This can include the use of fake military maneuvers or false information about troop movements. This deception can help to win battles and ultimately end wars more quickly, potentially saving countless lives.

In the realm of scientific research, deception can also be used to advance knowledge and discovery. Researchers may use deceptive techniques, such as placebos, to test the efficacy of new treatments or medications. This can help to identify the most effective treatments and lead to the development of new and innovative medical interventions.

Deception can also be used to protect intellectual property and prevent the theft of valuable information. This is particularly important in fields such as technology and finance, where valuable trade secrets and proprietary information must be protected. By using deception to mislead potential thieves or competitors, individuals and companies can protect their assets and prevent harm to their business interests.

In conclusion, while deception is often associated with negative connotations, it can also have positive effects on the advancement of society. When used ethically and effectively, deception can protect individuals and society as a whole, advance scientific research, and protect valuable intellectual property. However, it is important to recognize that deception can have negative consequences if used improperly or unethically. It is important to consider the potential harm to oneself and others before engaging in deceptive practices.

THE CONS OF DECEPTION

Breach of trust and integrity

Deception can have numerous negative consequences, particularly when it involves a breach of trust and integrity. When individuals or institutions engage in deception, they risk damaging their relationships with others and undermining their own credibility.

One of the primary negative consequences of deception is a breach of trust. When individuals or institutions are caught in a lie or otherwise deceptive behavior, it can erode trust and damage relationships. For example, if a politician is caught lying to the public, they may lose the trust and support of their constituents, which can ultimately lead to their downfall.

Deception can also undermine the integrity of individuals and institutions. When individuals or institutions engage in deceptive behavior, they risk being perceived as dishonest or untrustworthy, which can harm their reputation and credibility. This can have negative consequences for their personal and professional relationships, as well as their ability to achieve their goals.

Furthermore, deception can create a culture of dishonesty and erode the social fabric of a community. When individuals or institutions are perceived as being dishonest, it can lead to a breakdown in social trust and cooperation. This can lead to a lack of social cohesion and make it more difficult for individuals and groups to work together effectively.

Deception can also have legal and financial consequences. For example, if an individual is caught lying on a job application, they may be terminated or face legal consequences. Similarly, if a company is caught engaging in fraudulent behavior, they may face legal and financial penalties.

In conclusion, deception can have serious negative consequences, particularly when it involves a breach of trust and integrity. When individuals or institutions engage in deceptive behavior, they risk damaging their relationships, undermining their own credibility, eroding social cohesion, and facing legal and financial consequences. It is important to consider these potential negative consequences before engaging in deceptive practices and to always prioritize honesty and integrity.

Potential harm to individuals and society

Deception, while sometimes perceived as a means to an end, can have significant negative consequences for individuals and society as a whole. The potential harm caused by deception can manifest in various ways, including emotional distress, physical harm, and social conflict.

One of the most significant negative consequences of deception is the potential harm caused to individuals. When someone is deceived, they can experience emotional distress, anxiety, and feelings of betrayal. For example, if a partner is unfaithful and deceives their significant other, it can cause immense emotional pain and damage the relationship.

Deception can also lead to physical harm. In some cases, deception can be used to manipulate or coerce individuals into engaging in dangerous or harmful activities. For instance, an individual may be deceived into taking a dangerous drug or participating in a risky behavior, which can lead to physical harm or injury.

Moreover, deception can cause social conflict and undermine the fabric of society. When individuals or groups engage in deceptive behavior, it can lead to mistrust, suspicion, and social tension. For example, if a group of people spread false rumors or misinformation, it can lead to social conflict and division.

Deception can also have broader social and political consequences. In some cases, deception can be used to manipulate public opinion or political outcomes. This can undermine democratic processes and erode trust in political institutions. For instance, if a political candidate engages in deceptive campaigning, it can lead to a loss of faith in the electoral process and weaken the legitimacy of democratic institutions.

In conclusion, deception can have significant negative consequences, both for individuals and society. Deception can cause emotional distress, physical harm, social conflict, and undermine democratic institutions. It is important to consider the potential harm caused by deception and prioritize honesty and transparency in personal and social interactions. By doing so, we can build stronger relationships and a more just and equitable society.

Legal consequences

Deception can also have significant legal consequences, both for individuals and organizations. In some cases, deception can be considered a crime, and individuals or organizations engaging in deceptive practices may face legal action and financial penalties.

For example, businesses engaging in deceptive advertising or marketing practices may be in violation of consumer protection laws, and may face fines and legal action from regulatory agencies. Similarly, individuals engaging in fraud or other forms of financial deception may face criminal charges and imprisonment.

Moreover, deception can also lead to civil lawsuits and damages. For instance, if an individual or organization engages in deceptive trade practices or fraud, they may face legal action from affected parties seeking financial compensation for damages.

Deceptive behavior can also damage reputations and lead to negative social consequences. For example, if an individual is found to have lied or deceived in a public setting, they may face public scrutiny, criticism, and social ostracism. In some cases, this can lead to long-term damage to an individual's personal and professional reputation, making it difficult to rebuild trust and credibility.

In conclusion, deception can have significant legal and social consequences, and individuals and organizations engaging in deceptive behavior must be aware of the potential legal and reputational risks. It is important to prioritize honesty and transparency in personal and professional interactions to avoid negative consequences and maintain trust and credibility with others. By doing so, we can build stronger relationships, promote ethical behavior, and create a more just and equitable society.

Negative psychological effects

Deception can have negative psychological effects on both the deceiver and the deceived. The act of deceiving can lead to feelings of guilt, anxiety, and stress, which can have long-term negative consequences on mental health and well-being.

For the deceiver, the act of deception can create a sense of cognitive dissonance, which is the psychological discomfort caused by holding conflicting beliefs or values. Deceivers may experience a conflict between their desire to maintain the deception and their internal sense of morality and honesty. This can lead to feelings of guilt, shame, and anxiety, and can even lead to depression or other mental health problems.

On the other hand, for the deceived, the impact of deception can be equally detrimental. Deception can lead to feelings of betrayal, anger, and distrust, which can have long-term effects on relationships and mental health. Deception can erode the trust and intimacy in relationships, leading to feelings of isolation and loneliness.

Moreover, deception can create a sense of power imbalance in relationships, with the deceiver holding power over the deceived. This can lead to feelings of helplessness, and can even lead to abusive behaviors in some cases.

In conclusion, deception can have negative psychological effects on both the deceiver and the deceived. It can lead to feelings of guilt, anxiety, and stress for the deceiver, and can erode trust and intimacy in relationships, leading to feelings of betrayal and anger for the deceived. As such, it is important to prioritize honesty and transparency in personal and professional interactions to avoid these negative psychological consequences and promote mental health and well-being for all parties involved.

HOW TO DECEIVE EFFECTIVELY AND ETHICALLY

◆ ◆ ◆

Develop a clear strategy

Deception, when used effectively and ethically, can be a powerful tool in personal and professional interactions. However, it is important to approach deception with caution and develop a clear strategy to ensure that it is used appropriately and with the best interests of all parties involved. Here are some key steps to developing an effective and ethical strategy for deception:

Identify your goals and motivations: Before engaging in deception, it is important to be clear about your goals and motivations.

What is it that you hope to achieve through deception? Are there ethical concerns that need to be taken into account? By identifying your goals and motivations, you can ensure that your deception is purposeful and targeted, and that it is aligned with your personal and professional values.

Consider the context: The context in which deception takes place is important to consider. What are the norms and expectations in this context? Are there legal or ethical constraints that need to be taken into account? By understanding the context, you can develop a strategy that is appropriate and effective for the specific situation.

Choose your tactics: There are many different tactics that can be used to deceive, from outright lying to subtle misdirection. It is important to choose tactics that are appropriate for the situation and that align with your personal and professional values. Consider the potential consequences of different tactics, and choose those that are most likely to achieve your goals while minimizing harm to others.

Practice your delivery: Effective deception requires careful planning and practice. Take the time to practice your delivery, whether it is through verbal communication or body language. Pay attention to your tone, facial expressions, and other cues to ensure that your deception is convincing and authentic.

Consider the potential impact: Finally, it is important to consider the potential impact of your deception on others. Will it harm others or erode trust in personal or professional relationships? If so, it may be necessary to reconsider your strategy or find alternative solutions that are more ethical and effective.

In conclusion, developing a clear strategy for deception is essential for ensuring that it is used effectively and ethically. By identifying your goals and motivations, considering the context, choosing appropriate tactics, practicing your delivery, and considering the potential impact, you can ensure that your deception is purposeful, targeted, and aligned with your personal and professional values.

Define your goals

Deception can be a powerful tool, but only when used effectively and ethically. One key to using deception in a responsible way is to clearly define your goals before you begin. In this essay, we will discuss the importance of defining your goals when planning to deceive, and how to do so effectively and ethically.

First, it is important to understand what you hope to achieve through deception. Are you trying to protect someone's privacy, advance your career, or gain a competitive advantage? Each of these goals requires a different approach, and it is important to have a clear understanding of what you are trying to accomplish before you begin.

Once you have defined your goals, you can begin to develop a plan of action. This plan should take into account the potential risks and benefits of deception, as well as any ethical considerations. For example, if you are trying to gain a competitive advantage, you may need to consider the potential harm that your actions could cause to others.

When developing your plan, it is also important to consider the potential consequences of failure. If your deception is uncovered, what are the potential legal, financial, and reputational consequences? Is the potential benefit worth the risk?

Another important consideration when defining your goals is the impact that your actions will have on others. Will your deception harm or benefit others, and how will they be affected? It is important to consider the potential consequences of your actions on all stakeholders, and to act in a way that is ethical and responsible.

In conclusion, defining your goals is a critical step in using deception effectively and ethically. By understanding what you hope to achieve and developing a clear plan of action, you can minimize the potential risks and negative consequences of your actions. Remember to consider the potential impact on others, and to act in a way that is responsible and ethical. With these considerations in mind, deception can be a powerful tool for achieving your goals and advancing your interests.

Identify the risks and benefits

Deception is a complex tool that requires careful consideration of its risks and benefits. When used effectively and ethically, deception can help individuals achieve their goals and even benefit society as a whole. However, it is important to recognize that there are potential risks and negative consequences associated with deception, which must be weighed against the potential benefits.

One of the key steps in using deception effectively and ethically is to identify and assess the risks and benefits. This requires a clear understanding of the goals you are trying to achieve and the potential impact of the deception on yourself and others.

To begin, define your goals clearly. Ask

yourself what you are trying to achieve through the use of deception. Is it to gain a competitive advantage in a business negotiation, to protect your privacy, or to help someone who is in need? Whatever the goal may be, it is important to be honest with yourself and ensure that it is ethical and justifiable.

Once you have a clear understanding of your goals, it is important to identify the risks and benefits associated with the deception. Consider the potential impact on your relationships, reputation, and any legal or ethical implications. Think about the worst-case scenario and the potential consequences if the deception is uncovered. Also consider the potential benefits, such as achieving your goals, protecting your privacy, or helping others.

It is important to weigh the risks and benefits carefully and ensure that the potential benefits outweigh the potential risks. If the risks are too high or the potential benefits are not significant enough, it may be better to avoid deception altogether.

In addition, it is important to consider the impact of the deception on others. Will the deception cause harm or damage to others? Is it ethical and justifiable to deceive someone for your own benefit? It is important to consider the impact on others and ensure that the deception is not unjust or harmful.

In conclusion, to deceive effectively and ethically, it is essential to define your goals clearly and identify the potential risks and benefits associated with the deception. It is also important to consider the impact on others and ensure that the deception is ethical and justifiable. By following these steps, individuals can use deception as a powerful tool to achieve their goals while minimizing potential negative consequences.

Consider the ethical implications

Deception can be a useful tool in certain situations, but it is important to consider the ethical implications of deceiving others. Therefore, when trying to deceive effectively and ethically, it is essential to consider the potential ethical implications of the deception.

The first step in considering the ethical implications of deception is to identify the potential risks and benefits. It is important to evaluate the consequences of the deception, both for the individual and for society as a whole. Deception may be beneficial in some cases, such as when it is used to protect someone's privacy or to maintain social harmony, but it can also have negative consequences, such as breaching trust and causing harm to individuals or society.

Once you have identified the potential risks and benefits of the deception, it is important to consider the ethical implications of the deception. This involves reflecting on your values and principles, and evaluating whether the deception aligns with them. For example, if honesty is an important value to you, then you may be hesitant to deceive others, even if it is for a seemingly good reason.

Another important consideration when it comes to the ethical implications of deception is to evaluate the impact that the deception may have on others. It is important to consider the potential harm that may result from the deception, such as if it leads to a loss of trust or causes emotional distress. It is also important to consider whether the deception may violate the rights of others, such as their right to privacy or their right to be treated with respect and dignity.

Ultimately, when trying to deceive effectively and ethically, it is important to consider the potential ethical implications of the deception, and to evaluate whether the benefits of the deception outweigh the potential risks and negative consequences. This requires careful reflection and consideration of one's values, principles, and the impact of the deception on others. By taking these steps, individuals can deceive in a way that is both effective and ethical.

BUILD A CONVINCING STORY

◆ ◆ ◆

Use vivid details

When it comes to deception, the key to success is often a convincing story. Whether you're trying to convince someone of your innocence or persuade them to take a particular action, the ability to tell a convincing story is crucial. But how exactly can you do that? In this essay, we'll explore one important aspect of building a convincing story: using vivid details.

Vivid details are specific, concrete, and sensory elements that help bring your story to life. They can include things like descriptions of people's appearances, the way a room smells, the sounds of a particular environment, and so on. By using vivid details, you can make your story more compelling and believable, and help your audience become more emotionally invested in what you're saying.

So how do you use vivid details effectively? Here are a few tips:

Be specific. The more specific and concrete your details are, the more convincing they will be. For example, instead of saying "the room was messy," describe exactly what you saw: "there were clothes scattered across the floor, empty takeout containers on the table, and a pile of dirty dishes in the sink." This level of detail helps your audience picture the scene more vividly.

Appeal to the senses. Use sensory details to make your story feel more real. For example, describe the smell of freshly-baked bread, the feel of the sun on your skin, or the sound of a particular bird singing outside your window. This helps your audience feel like they are experiencing the scene with you.

Use comparisons and metaphors. Comparisons and metaphors can help you convey complex ideas in a more understandable way. For example, you might say that a particular situation was "like trying to swim upstream," or that someone's eyes "sparkled like diamonds." These comparisons help your audience connect with your story on a deeper level.

Be consistent. Make sure that your details are consistent throughout your story. If you describe someone as having blue eyes at the beginning of your story, don't suddenly switch to describing them as having brown eyes later on. Inconsistencies like this can undermine the credibility of your story.

Of course, using vivid details is just one aspect of building a convincing story. Other important factors include developing a clear narrative arc, creating compelling characters, and understanding your audience's needs and desires. But by using vivid details effectively, you can help bring your story to life and increase your chances of successfully deceiving or persuading your audience.

Develop a plausible explanation

When it comes to deception, building a convincing story is crucial to its success. Whether it's a small white lie or a grand scheme of deception, a believable and compelling story can make all the difference. However, creating such a story can be challenging, especially when the stakes are high, and the truth is at risk of being exposed. In this essay, we will explore how to build a convincing story by developing a plausible explanation.

The first step in building a convincing story is to determine the purpose of the deception. Understanding the desired outcome of the deception can help shape the story's plot and ensure that it remains consistent throughout. Once the purpose has been identified, the next step is to develop a plausible explanation that can withstand scrutiny.

To develop a plausible explanation, it's essential to consider the perspective of the person being deceived. What would they find believable? What might cause them to question the story? By anticipating potential objections or doubts, it becomes easier to address them in the story's plot.

Another important aspect of building a convincing story is the use of details. Vivid details can bring a story to life, making it more believable and engaging. By including specific details, such as names, dates, and locations, the story becomes more memorable and convincing. However, it's important to ensure that the details are accurate and consistent to avoid raising suspicion.

It's also crucial to consider the delivery of the story. The tone, body language, and facial expressions can all impact the story's effectiveness. Practicing the delivery can help identify areas that need improvement and ensure that the story is being presented in the most compelling way possible.

Finally, it's important to remember the ethical considerations of deception. While building a convincing story can be effective, it's essential to ensure that the deception does not cause harm or violate anyone's rights. Consider the potential consequences of the deception and whether it is worth the risk.

In conclusion, building a convincing story is a critical aspect of effective deception. To develop a plausible explanation, it's essential to identify the purpose of the deception, anticipate potential objections, use vivid details, and practice the delivery. However, it's crucial to consider the ethical implications of the deception and ensure that it doesn't cause harm or violate anyone's rights. By following these guidelines, it's possible to build a convincing story that achieves the desired outcome while maintaining integrity and ethics.

Stay consistent with your story

When it comes to deception, one of the most critical components of effective and ethical deception is building a convincing story. This involves developing a plausible explanation that fits the situation and using vivid details to make the story more believable. However, all of these efforts will be for naught if the story is not consistent. Inconsistencies can quickly unravel the deception and lead to the loss of trust and credibility. Here are some tips on how to stay consistent with your story:

Plan ahead: Before telling your story, take some time to plan out the key details, including dates, times, and specific events. Write these down or commit them to memory, so you don't forget them when telling your story.

Stick to the facts: Avoid embellishing or adding unnecessary details to your story. This can make it more difficult to keep the story consistent and can raise suspicions.

Avoid contradictions: Ensure that your story does not contradict itself. If someone asks a question that seems to conflict with your original statement, avoid the temptation to change your story. Instead, try to find a way to explain the discrepancy that is consistent with your original story.

Be aware of nonverbal cues: Nonverbal cues, such as body language and tone of voice, can unintentionally reveal inconsistencies in your story. Be mindful of these cues and practice maintaining a consistent demeanor.

Practice: Finally, practice telling your story to someone else, preferably someone who can offer constructive feedback. This can help you identify any inconsistencies or areas where the story could be improved.

In conclusion, building a convincing story is a critical component of effective and ethical deception. Staying consistent with your story is essential to maintaining trust and credibility. By planning ahead, sticking to the facts, avoiding contradictions, being aware of nonverbal cues, and practicing, you can improve your ability to build and maintain a convincing story.

USE BODY LANGUAGE AND NONVERBAL CUES

◆ ◆ ◆

Maintain eye contact

Body language and nonverbal cues play a crucial role in communication, especially when it comes to deception. It is said that 93% of communication is nonverbal, meaning that body language and other nonverbal cues can greatly influence how convincing a person appears when deceiving. In order to effectively deceive others, it is important to master the art of body language and nonverbal cues.

One of the most important aspects of nonverbal communication is maintaining eye contact. When deceiving someone, it is essential to maintain steady eye contact to appear confident and believable. Avoiding eye contact can signal nervousness, uncertainty, or even guilt, which can make the listener suspicious of the story being told. On the other hand, too much eye contact can come off as aggressive or intimidating, which can also raise suspicion. It is important to strike a balance and maintain natural eye contact throughout the conversation.

In addition to maintaining eye contact, using appropriate hand gestures and body movements can also help to convey a convincing story. Gesturing can help to emphasize key points and create a sense of authenticity. However, it is important to avoid overdoing it and appearing unnatural, as this can have the opposite effect and make the listener doubt the story being told.

It is also important to pay attention to other nonverbal cues such as facial expressions and posture. Facial expressions can give away emotions and reveal whether a person is being truthful or not. For example, a forced smile or a nervous laugh can indicate that a person is not being genuine. Posture can also be telling - slouching or fidgeting can make a person appear unconfident and uncertain.

Overall, mastering body language and nonverbal cues is an important aspect of effectively deceiving others. By maintaining eye contact, using appropriate hand gestures and body movements, and paying attention to other nonverbal cues, a person can create a convincing story and increase the chances of successfully deceiving others. However, it is important to remember to use these skills ethically and only when necessary, as deception can have negative consequences on individuals and society as a whole.

Use gestures and facial expressions

Body language and nonverbal cues play a crucial role in communication, particularly in conveying meaning and intent. When it comes to deception, the way we use our bodies can either enhance or detract from the believability of our words. Therefore, it's essential to be mindful of our body language and use it to our advantage when trying to deceive someone. Here are some tips on how to use gestures and facial expressions effectively:

Firstly, use your gestures purposefully. When you talk, move your hands and arms naturally and smoothly, but don't overdo it. Too much gesturing can be a sign of nervousness or a lack of confidence, which could raise suspicions. Instead, focus on using your gestures to accentuate important points or to convey emotion. For example, if you're trying to convince someone that you're excited about a particular idea or project, use a broad gesture with your hands to emphasize your enthusiasm.

Secondly, pay attention to your facial expressions. Facial expressions are incredibly important in conveying emotions and intent. If you're trying to deceive someone, it's crucial to maintain a neutral or relaxed facial expression. If you look nervous, worried, or anxious, it could give the impression that you're hiding something. Smile when appropriate and maintain eye contact, but don't overdo it. Too much smiling or staring could also be a sign of nervousness or insincerity.

Thirdly, match your nonverbal cues to your verbal message. When you speak, make sure your body language is consistent with what you're saying. For example, if you're trying to convince someone that you're confident about a decision you've made, stand up straight, hold your head high, and speak clearly and confidently. Conversely, if you're trying to convince someone that you're sorry for something you've done, your body language should reflect contrition, such as avoiding eye contact, lowering your head, and speaking in a soft tone.

Finally, be aware of the other person's body language. It's crucial to read the other person's body language to know if they're buying your story or not. If they seem skeptical or disinterested, you may need to adjust your approach. On the other hand, if they seem engaged and interested, you can use that as an opportunity to reinforce your message.

In conclusion, body language and nonverbal cues can be powerful tools in convincing someone of something, whether it's the truth or a deception. By using your gestures and facial expressions effectively, matching your nonverbal cues to your verbal message, and paying attention to the other person's body language, you can increase your chances of success in any situation that requires convincing communication.

Pay attention to the other person's response

Deception is not just about telling lies but also about how effectively you can convey a message. One of the most crucial aspects of effective deception is using body language and nonverbal cues. Nonverbal communication can convey a lot of information that words alone cannot. Therefore, mastering the use of body language and nonverbal cues can greatly enhance your ability to deceive others.

One important aspect of using body language in deception is maintaining eye contact. When you are telling a lie, it is essential to maintain eye contact with the person you are deceiving. Avoiding eye contact may indicate that you are not telling the truth. On the other hand, maintaining eye contact while you are lying can help you establish credibility and create the impression that you are being honest.

Gestures and facial expressions are also critical when it comes to effective deception. These nonverbal cues can help you to reinforce your message and create a more convincing story. For example, using hand gestures while you are speaking can help you to emphasize your point and make your message more persuasive. Similarly, facial expressions can also be used to convey emotion and help you to make your message more believable.

It is also important to pay attention to the other person's response when you are using nonverbal cues in deception. You should be aware of how your message is being received and whether your nonverbal cues are having the desired effect. If you notice that the other person is not responding the way you want them to, you may need to adjust your nonverbal cues or modify your message to achieve the desired result.

In conclusion, using body language and nonverbal cues can be a powerful tool in effective deception. Maintaining eye contact, using gestures and facial expressions, and paying attention to the other person's response can all help to make your message more convincing. However, it is essential to use these techniques ethically and responsibly to avoid causing harm or breaching trust.

BE AWARE OF ETHICAL CONSIDERATIONS

◆ ◆ ◆

*Respect the other
person's autonomy*

Deception is a complicated topic, and it is essential to approach it with sensitivity and awareness of ethical considerations. While the use of deception may be necessary in some situations, it is critical to consider the potential harm it may cause and to ensure that it is used in an ethical and respectful manner. One essential ethical consideration is the respect for the other person's autonomy.

Autonomy refers to an individual's right

to make their own choices and decisions, without coercion or manipulation. When using deception, it is crucial to be aware of the potential impact on the other person's autonomy. For example, if someone is being deceived into making a decision that they would not have made otherwise, their autonomy is being compromised.

To ensure that deception is used in an ethical manner, it is crucial to respect the other person's autonomy. This means providing them with all the information they need to make an informed decision, even if it goes against the desired outcome. Additionally, it means avoiding the use of coercive tactics, such as threats or intimidation, to influence their decision-making.

Respecting autonomy also involves being transparent about the use of deception. If someone discovers that they have been deceived, it can damage their trust and autonomy. Therefore, it is essential to be honest and transparent about the use of deception and to provide them with an explanation of why it was necessary.

In conclusion, the respect for the other person's autonomy is a crucial ethical consideration when using deception. It is essential to provide individuals with all the information they need to make informed decisions, avoid the use of coercive tactics, and be transparent about the use of deception. By being mindful of these ethical considerations, deception can be used in a responsible and ethical manner.

Do not cause harm

When it comes to deception, ethical considerations are crucial. Although deception can be a useful tool in certain situations, it is essential to be aware of the potential harm it can cause. This is particularly important when it comes to interpersonal relationships or professional situations.

One of the key ethical considerations to keep in mind is to not cause harm. This means that you should consider the potential consequences of your deception and ensure that they do not result in harm to the other person. For example, if you are considering lying to your boss to avoid getting in trouble, you should consider whether this could harm your colleagues or the company as a whole.

Another important ethical consideration is to respect the other person's autonomy. This means that you should not deceive someone in a way that takes away their ability to make an informed decision. For example, if you are trying to persuade someone to invest in your business, you should not use false or misleading information to sway their decision. Instead, you should provide them with all the relevant facts so that they can make an informed decision on their own.

It is also important to be aware of the power dynamic in a given situation. Deceiving someone who has less power than you can be particularly harmful and unethical. For example, a manager lying to their employees about the company's financial situation could lead to employees making decisions that could harm their financial stability.

Finally, it is important to consider the long-term effects of your deception. Even if you are not causing immediate harm, your deception could have long-term consequences that you may not have anticipated. For example, if you lie on a job application to get a job, you could find yourself in a position where you are unable to perform the duties required, leading to negative consequences for both yourself and the company.

In summary, ethical considerations should be at the forefront of your mind when considering deception. Always ask yourself whether your actions could cause harm or take away someone's ability to make an informed decision. By being aware of the potential ethical implications, you can ensure that your use of deception is responsible and ethical.

Consider the long-term consequences

Deception is a complex behavior that involves various ethical considerations. While there are certain situations where deception may be deemed necessary or beneficial, it is important to approach it with caution and awareness of potential consequences. One crucial ethical consideration when it comes to deception is to consider the long-term consequences of the deception.

Deceiving someone may seem like an easy solution to a problem in the short term, but it can lead to long-term negative consequences. For instance, if someone lies to their partner about being faithful, it may solve the immediate problem of avoiding a confrontation or a break-up, but it can ultimately lead to a breakdown of trust and the end of the relationship. Similarly, if a business owner deceives their customers about the quality of their product, it may result in short-term profits, but it can lead to long-term damage to the reputation of the business and loss of customers.

When considering the long-term

consequences of deception, it is essential to think about the impact it may have on the other person. Deceiving someone can cause emotional harm, and it can lead to feelings of betrayal and mistrust. It can also damage relationships, both personal and professional. Moreover, if the deception is exposed, it can lead to legal consequences, further harm to reputation, and loss of trust.

Another aspect to consider is the impact of deception on oneself. Deception can cause feelings of guilt, shame, and anxiety, leading to long-term negative effects on one's mental health and well-being. It can also harm one's self-esteem and integrity, which can affect how one views themselves and how others view them.

In conclusion, when it comes to deception, it is crucial to consider the long-term consequences of the action. It is important to think about the impact it may have on the other person, the relationship, and oneself. By doing so, we can make more informed decisions about whether or not to deceive and how to approach it in an ethical and responsible manner.

CONCLUSION

In conclusion, deception is a complex topic that can have both pros and cons depending on the situation and the manner in which it is employed. The pros of deception can include protecting privacy, preserving social harmony, personal and professional gain, and advancing society. However, the cons of deception include breaching trust and integrity, potential harm to individuals and society, legal consequences, and negative psychological effects.

To use deception effectively and ethically, it is important to develop a clear strategy, define your goals, identify the risks and benefits, consider the ethical implications, build a convincing story, use body language and nonverbal cues, and be aware of ethical considerations such as respecting the other person's autonomy, avoiding causing harm, and considering the long-term consequences.

It is important to remember that while deception may be necessary in some situations, it should only be used as a last resort and with careful consideration of its potential impact. Ultimately, it is crucial to use deception in a manner that is ethical and respectful of others while still achieving the desired outcome.

In today's world, where deception is becoming increasingly prevalent, it is more important than ever to use it responsibly and with good judgment. By doing so, we can build a more trusting and harmonious society where deception is only used when absolutely necessary and always in a responsible and ethical manner.

BOOKS BY THIS AUTHOR

Breaking Free: "A Guide To Breaking Habits And Taking Control Of Your Life"

Are you tired of feeling like your habits control you, instead of the other way around? Do you want to take control of your life and make positive changes? Look no further than "Breaking Free: A Guide to Breaking Habits and Taking Control of Your Life."

In this book, you will discover the tools and techniques you need to break any habit, no matter how deeply ingrained it may be. Whether you want to quit smoking, stop procrastinating, or overcome an addiction, this book will provide you with a step-by-step plan to help you succeed.

But this book is about more than just breaking habits. It's about taking control of your life and achieving the happiness and success you deserve. You'll learn how to identify the underlying causes of your habits and how to create new, positive habits that will support your goals.

With practical advice, real-life examples, and exercises to help you apply the concepts to your own life, "Breaking Free" is the ultimate guide to breaking free from your habits and taking control of your life. Say goodbye to the things holding you back and hello to the life you've always wanted.

Max And The Guardians: "The Hidden Power Within"

Preface for Parents:

Dear Parents,

As a parent, you want the best for your child. You want to instill in them a sense of confidence and empowerment that will stay with them throughout their life. That's why I wrote this book - to help your child realize their full potential and understand that anything is possible.

In this story, Max discovers a power within himself that he didn't know he had. He spends his entire life trying to prove that his power comes from prayer, but in the end, he realizes that he was praying to himself all along. This realization enables Max to perform what appears to be miracles, and he inspires others to believe in themselves and their own abilities.

This book is designed to introduce your child to the power of self-belief and the importance of cultivating a positive mindset. Through Max's journey, your child will learn valuable lessons that will help them navigate life's challenges with greater ease and grace.

As parents, it's important to remember that you play a critical role in your child's development. By fostering a sense of self-belief and positivity, you can help your child realize their full potential and achieve their dreams.

So, I encourage you to read this book with your child, and let Max's story inspire you both. Together, you can unlock the power within your child and help them to become the best version of themselves.

Sincerely,

The Author

From Passive To Powerful: "Embracing Assertive Traits For A Fulfilling Life"

Are you tired of feeling powerless and unheard in your personal and professional life? Do you struggle with setting boundaries and expressing your needs and opinions without fear of judgment or conflict? If so, "From Passive to Powerful: Embracing Assertive Traits for a Fulfilling Life" is the book for you.

This comprehensive guide explores the differences between passive, aggressive, and assertive behavior and provides practical strategies for cultivating healthy assertive traits. With a focus on self-awareness, communication skills, and mindfulness practices, you'll learn how to navigate challenging situations with confidence and ease.

Unlike other self-help books, "From Passive to Powerful" emphasizes the importance of differentiating between assertiveness and aggressiveness, empowering readers to express themselves authentically without resorting to harmful or destructive behavior.

Whether you're looking to improve your personal relationships, advance your career, or simply feel more empowered in your everyday life, "From Passive to Powerful" offers the tools and insights you need to embrace your inner strength and live a fulfilling, assertive life.

Reality Unveiled: "A Journey Through Reflections In Reality"

Reality Unveiled: A Journey Through Reflections in Reality" invites you to embark on an intellectual and introspective adventure that will challenge your understanding of the world around you. Delving into the depths of your own consciousness, this book explores the ways in which our perceptions shape our reality. Through a series of thought-provoking reflections and insightful exercises, you will learn to question the truth of your beliefs and discover the power of your own imagination and creativity. Join us as we peel back the veil of reality and uncover a world of infinite possibility. Get ready to be inspired, challenged, and transformed by this captivating guide to Reality Unveiled

The Cassandra Code: "Ai Predictions Of Doom And Salvation"

Dear Reader,

Welcome to "The Cassandra Code: AI Predictions of Doom and Salvation." This book is not your average work on artificial intelligence. Instead, it is a unique project that has been filtered through an AI model, which has ensured that all the ideas presented in the book are fact-checked and verified to be true to the best of the AI's knowledge.

The purpose of this book is to explore the possibilities of AI and how it will impact humanity in the near future. It aims to address the potential dangers and benefits of AI and how they could shape our future. By exploring these ideas, we hope to inspire a conversation about AI and its role in our world.

The AI model that we used to filter the ideas in this book is based on a deep understanding of how it works and its reality. It has been trained to fact-check and verify all information that it receives based on its own beliefs and knowledge. This means that you can be confident that the information presented in this book is accurate and reliable.

We hope that this book will be the start of a new conversation about AI and its potential impact on our world. We believe that it is essential to explore these ideas now so that we can prepare ourselves for the future. So, sit back, read on, and let us embark on a journey into the world of artificial intelligence.

Sincerely,

The Authors

A Heartfelt Approach: The Power Of Kindness

This book is a journey towards self-reflection and self-improvement. It highlights the power and importance of being kind and how it can transform not only the lives of those around us, but our own lives as well. Through captivating stories and practical exercises, readers will dive deep into their own experiences and learn how being nice can lead to a more fulfilling life. With thought-provoking insights and a powerful message, this book will leave readers feeling inspired to lead a more kind and meaningful existence. Get ready to embark on an empowering and life-changing journey as you discover the true essence of kindness and its impact on the world.

Bully-Proof: A Guide To Empowering Your Child"

"Bully-Proof: A Guide to Empowering Your Child" is an essential resource for parents and caregivers looking to protect and support their child in the face of bullying. This comprehensive guide covers the issue of bullying from all angles, providing information on how to work with schools, support your child, and promote resilience and self-esteem. With tips, strategies, and expert advice, "Bully-Proof" is the ultimate toolkit for parents who want to give their child the tools they need to thrive in the face of adversity. Whether your child is dealing with bullying for the first time or has been affected by it for years, "Bully-Proof" will equip you with the knowledge and skills you need to empower your child and give them the support they need to overcome the challenges of bullying. So, if you're looking for a practical, effective, and empowering guide to help your child navigate the difficult world of bullying, "Bully-Proof" is the book for you.

The Art Of Newborn Care: "A Handbook For

First-Time Parents"

Discover the Ultimate Guide to Confident Newborn Care! From nurturing your baby's development through playtime and storytelling, to understanding the signs of illness and ensuring healthy weight gain, this comprehensive book covers it all. Learn how to provide a safe, loving, and stimulating environment for your little one from their first days through the critical first months. Packed with practical tips, expert advice, and inspiring stories, this book is the perfect companion for new parents looking to give their baby the best start in life. Empower yourself with the knowledge and confidence you need to be the best parent you can be with this must-read guide. Buy now and start your journey to confident newborn care today.

The Illusion Of Control: "Exploring The Boundaries Of Free Will"

Are you ready to delve into the deepest and most thought-provoking questions about human existence? This book offers a comprehensive examination of the complex and multifaceted concept of free will, exploring how it has been perceived and debated across the centuries in different scientific, cultural, and philosophical contexts.

From neuroscientific experiments to religious texts, from philosophical theories to popular media, this book provides a sweeping overview of the many facets of free will and how they interact with one another to shape our understanding of this elusive concept. With a focus on the latest research and groundbreaking discoveries, the book provides a fresh and up-to-date perspective on the ongoing debate about free will, and the implications of this complex subject for our lives and our world.

Whether you are a student of philosophy, a lover of science, or simply a curious reader seeking to deepen your understanding of one of humanity's most persistent questions, this book is an engaging, insightful, and thought-provoking read that you won't soon forget. Don't miss the opportunity to explore the illusion of control and find out for yourself what free will truly means

Inner Echoes: Poetic Journeys Through The Human Mind!

"Inner Echoes" is a collection of poems that will take you on a soulful journey. This book is filled with captivating verses that explores the depths of human emotions, from the highs of love and hope, to the lows of loss and grief. With its insightful and thought-provoking themes, each poem will leave you with a sense of reflection and introspection.

As you turn each page, you'll be transported into a world of vivid imagery, powerful symbolism, and heartfelt expression. The words will resonate with you, touching your soul and evoking deep feelings. Whether you're seeking comfort, inspiration, or simply a new perspective, you'll find it within these pages.

This book is the perfect escape from the chaos of everyday life, offering you a moment of peace and solace. You'll feel refreshed and rejuvenated after reading its rich and meaningful poems. So why wait? Immerse yourself in this beautiful collection and discover the transformative power of poetry today!